The Art of Gourmet Cuisine: The Ultimate Gourmet Cuisine Cookbook

Harper Baker

Copyright © 2023 by Harper Baker

All rights reserved. No part of this publication may be reproduced, distributed, or transmitted in any form or by any means, including photocopying, recording, or other electronic or mechanical methods, without the prior written permission of the publisher, except in the case of brief quotations embodied in critical reviews and certain other noncommercial uses permitted by copyright law.

This book is sold subject to the condition that it shall not, by way of trade or otherwise, be lent, re-sold, hired out, or otherwise circulated without the publisher's prior consent in any form of binding or cover other than that in which it is published and without a similar condition, including this condition, being imposed on the subsequent purchaser.

The information provided in this book is for general informational purposes only. While every effort has been made to ensure the accuracy and completeness of the information, the publisher and author assume no responsibility for errors or omissions, or for damages resulting from the use of the information contained herein.

Printed in the United States of America.

INTRODUCTION

Welcome to "The Art of Gourmet Cuisine: The Ultimate Gourmet Cuisine Cookbook," a culinary journey that will transport you into the realm of exquisite flavors, elegant presentations, and the mastery of gourmet cooking. In these pages, we invite you to explore the secrets and techniques that define the world of gastronomy at its finest.

Gourmet cuisine is an art form that goes beyond mere sustenance; it is an expression of passion, creativity, and attention to detail. It embraces the finest ingredients, the most delicate balance of flavors, and the artful presentation that transforms a meal into an unforgettable experience. Whether you are a seasoned chef or an enthusiastic home cook, this cookbook is your gateway to the enchanting world of gourmet cooking.

In this comprehensive guide, we have curated a collection of recipes that will inspire and challenge you, enabling you to create stunning dishes worthy of the most discerning palates. From the foundation techniques that form the backbone of gourmet cuisine to the innovative flavor combinations that push boundaries, each chapter is designed to expand your culinary horizons and elevate your skills to new heights.

Discover the art of infusing ingredients with depth and complexity, as well as the techniques used by renowned chefs to create symphonies of flavors. Unveil the secrets behind preparing succulent meats, delicate seafood, and vibrant vegetarian dishes. Dive into the world of sauces, dressings, and garnishes that add the perfect finishing touch to any gourmet creation. And, of course, indulge in the sweet delights of gourmet desserts and pastries that will leave a lasting impression on your taste buds.

Along this journey, you will find chapters dedicated to essential pantry ingredients, tips on sourcing the freshest produce, and guidance on mastering the art of food presentation. We aim to equip you with the knowledge and skills to confidently craft gourmet meals in your own kitchen, and to inspire you to unleash your own creativity and passion.

Whether you aspire to impress your guests at a special dinner party, create memorable family meals, or simply take your everyday cooking to the next level, "The Art of Gourmet Cuisine: The Ultimate Gourmet Cuisine Cookbook" is your indispensable companion. Embrace the challenge, embrace the artistry, and embark on a culinary adventure that will awaken your senses and transform the way you experience food.

Let us embark on this gastronomic voyage together, celebrating the beauty and artistry of gourmet cuisine. Prepare to unlock the door to a world of extraordinary flavors, culinary innovation, and pure epicurean delight. Welcome to the art of gourmet cuisine!

Table of Contents

Chapter 1   The Foundations of Gourmet Cooking: Techniques and Principles
Chapter 2   Unveiling the Gourmet Pantry: Essential Ingredients and Seasonings
Chapter 3   From Amuse-Bouche to Grand Entrées: Creating Stunning Appetizers
Chapter 4   Soups and Bisques: A Symphony of Flavors
Chapter 5   Exquisite Seafood Delights: Unleashing the Ocean's Bounty
Chapter 6   The Art of Meat: Mastering Gourmet Meat Cookery
Chapter 7   Poultry Perfection: Elevating Chicken, Duck, and Game Birds
Chapter 8   Sensational Sauces: Elevating Flavors to New Heights
Chapter 9   Decadent Pasta Creations: Fresh, Homemade, and Gourmet
Chapter 10   Vegetarian Gastronomy: Celebrating the Bounty of Nature
Chapter 11   Gourmet Grains and Legumes: Elevating Simple Staples
Chapter 12   Salads and Dressings: Innovative Combinations and Artful Presentations
Chapter 13   The Art of Cheese: Pairing and Presenting Fine Cheeses
Chapter 14   From Farm to Table: Embracing Locally Sourced Ingredients
Chapter 15   Culinary Fusion: Exploring Global Gourmet Flavors
Chapter 16   Sweet Temptations: Mastering Gourmet Desserts
Chapter 17   Artful Baking: Pies, Tarts, and Pastries
Chapter 18   Chocolatier's Delight: Crafting Divine Chocolate Creations

Chapter19 Gourmet Entertaining: Hosting Memorable Dinner Parties
Chapter20 The Art of Food Presentation: Plating Techniques and Garnishes

Chapter 1

The Foundations of Gourmet Cooking: Techniques and Principles

In the world of gourmet cooking, technique is the cornerstone upon which culinary excellence is built. This chapter delves into the essential techniques and principles that form the foundation of gourmet cuisine. From knife skills and cooking methods to flavor development and plating techniques, mastering these fundamentals will empower you to create extraordinary dishes that embody the artistry of gourmet cooking.

Knife Skills: The art of precision
No gourmet kitchen is complete without honed knife skills. A sharp and well-maintained knife, coupled with proper cutting techniques, is crucial for achieving consistent and professional results. Learn the various knife cuts, from julienne to chiffonade, and understand how they contribute to texture, presentation, and even cooking times. Discover the importance of proper knife grip, hand positioning, and the art of honing and sharpening your blades.

Cooking Methods: Harnessing the power of heat
Gourmet cuisine embraces a diverse range of cooking methods, each offering unique opportunities for flavor development and texture manipulation. Explore techniques such as sautéing, braising, roasting, and sous vide. Learn when to use high heat to sear and caramelize, or low and slow to tenderize and infuse flavors. Understand the art of deglazing, reducing, and creating rich sauces to elevate your dishes.

Flavor Development: Building complexity

Gourmet cooking is all about layering flavors and creating harmonious taste profiles. Dive into the principles of seasoning, balancing acidity, and incorporating umami-rich ingredients. Discover the art of creating aromatic bases, such as mirepoix and sofrito, that serve as foundations for countless dishes. Experiment with herbs, spices, and aromatic ingredients to add depth and complexity to your culinary creations.

Ingredient Quality: Sourcing the finest
The essence of gourmet cuisine lies in the quality of ingredients used. Explore the importance of sourcing fresh, seasonal produce, sustainably raised meats, and ethically sourced seafood. Learn how to assess ingredient quality, select the best cuts of meat, and identify peak ripeness in fruits and vegetables. Discover the impact of ingredient quality on the overall taste and presentation of your gourmet dishes.

Presentation Techniques: Artistry on the plate
Plating is an integral aspect of gourmet cooking, where culinary creations are transformed into works of art. Delve into the principles of plate composition, balance, and visual appeal. Learn about color harmony, texture contrast, and the strategic placement of elements to create visually stunning dishes. Discover techniques for elegant garnishes, such as microgreens, edible flowers, and delicate sauce drizzles, that elevate the presentation of your gourmet creations.

The Science of Cooking: Understanding the why
Gourmet cooking is not just an art; it is also a science. Explore the underlying scientific principles that influence cooking, such as heat transfer, protein denaturation, and emulsion formation. Understand the Maillard reaction and caramelization, and how they contribute to flavor development and browning. Discover how understanding the

science behind cooking can enhance your ability to troubleshoot and innovate in the kitchen.

Culinary Etiquette: The art of dining
Gourmet cuisine is often associated with refined dining experiences. Familiarize yourself with dining etiquette, table settings, and proper service techniques. Learn about wine pairing principles, including selecting the right wine varietals to complement your gourmet dishes. Gain insights into the art of creating memorable dining experiences, from ambiance and lighting to music selection and creating a welcoming atmosphere for your guests.

Conclusion:

Mastering the techniques and principles of gourmet cooking is an ongoing journey that requires dedication, practice, and a deep appreciation for the culinary arts. In this chapter, we have laid the groundwork for your gourmet adventure, equipping you with the knowledge and skills necessary to embark on this extraordinary culinary path. As you refine your knife skills, experiment with cooking methods, and explore the science behind cooking, remember that the foundations you build today will serve as the springboard for your future gourmet creations. So, let us embark on this quest for culinary excellence together, armed with the techniques and principles that will enable you to create extraordinary gourmet dishes that leave a lasting impression on those fortunate enough to experience them.

Chapter 2

Unveiling the Gourmet Pantry: Essential Ingredients and Seasonings

A well-stocked pantry is the heart and soul of gourmet cooking. In this chapter, we dive into the world of essential ingredients and seasonings that elevate your dishes from ordinary to extraordinary. Discover the key elements that form the backbone of gourmet cuisine, from aromatic herbs and spices to flavorful oils and vinegars. Unveil the secrets of building a gourmet pantry, where each ingredient plays a vital role in enhancing taste, aroma, and complexity.

Aromatic Herbs: Fragrant essences of flavor
Aromatic herbs are the building blocks of gourmet cuisine, imparting depth, fragrance, and nuance to dishes. Explore the world of herbs such as rosemary, thyme, basil, and tarragon. Learn the art of incorporating fresh herbs into your cooking, from delicate garnishes to herb-infused oils and butters. Discover how to balance and combine different herbs to create tantalizing flavor profiles that elevate your gourmet creations.

Exquisite Spices: The keys to culinary magic
Spices add a touch of exotic allure to gourmet dishes, infusing them with complexity and intrigue. Delve into the realm of spices like cinnamon, cumin, cardamom, and star anise. Learn about the art of toasting and grinding spices to unlock their full potential. Experiment with spice blends and rubs, transforming ordinary ingredients into extraordinary culinary masterpieces. Discover the art of balancing spices to create harmonious flavor profiles that captivate the palate.

Flavorful Oils: Essence of richness

Gourmet cooking embraces a variety of oils, each contributing its unique flavor and characteristics. Explore the world of extra virgin olive oil, walnut oil, truffle oil, and more. Learn when to use each oil to enhance the taste and texture of your dishes. Discover the art of infusing oils with herbs, spices, and aromatics to create flavorful condiments and dressings. Understand the importance of selecting high-quality oils for optimum taste and health benefits.

Vinegars and Acids: Balancing acidity
Acidity is a crucial element in gourmet cooking, providing balance and brightness to dishes. Discover the diverse range of vinegars, such as balsamic, red wine, and apple cider vinegar. Learn how to incorporate vinegars into marinades, dressings, and reductions to elevate flavors. Explore the world of citrus juices and other acidic ingredients, understanding how they contribute to taste and the preservation of vibrant colors in gourmet cuisine.

Umami-rich Ingredients: The fifth taste sensation
Umami is the savory taste that adds depth and richness to gourmet dishes. Unveil the secrets of umami-rich ingredients, including soy sauce, miso, Parmesan cheese, and mushrooms. Learn how to harness the power of umami to create complex flavor profiles that leave a lasting impression. Discover the art of using umami ingredients as flavor enhancers, elevating the taste of sauces, stocks, and even desserts.

Specialty Ingredients: Exotic treasures
Gourmet cooking often involves incorporating specialty ingredients that add a touch of luxury and intrigue to dishes. Delve into the world of truffles, foie gras, saffron, and caviar. Learn how to use these ingredients judiciously to create unforgettable gourmet experiences. Understand their unique

characteristics, storage methods, and the art of pairing them with complementary flavors.

Preserved and Fermented Ingredients: Complexity and depth

Preserved and fermented ingredients are prized in gourmet cooking for their intense flavors and unique textures. Explore the realm of pickles, preserved lemons, kimchi, and fermented sauces like fish sauce and soy sauce. Learn how to incorporate these ingredients into your dishes to create depth, complexity, and a hint of tanginess. Understand the balance between acidity and umami that these ingredients bring to gourmet cuisine.

Artisanal and Local Ingredients: Celebrating regional flavors

Gourmet cuisine embraces the beauty of artisanal and locally sourced ingredients, celebrating the unique flavors of different regions. Discover the joys of working with artisanal cheeses, locally sourced honey, heirloom vegetables, and heritage grains. Learn how these ingredients contribute to the authenticity and terroir of your gourmet dishes. Gain insights into supporting local producers and fostering a sustainable approach to gourmet cooking.

Conclusion:

Building a well-stocked gourmet pantry is an essential step towards unlocking the full potential of your culinary prowess. By exploring the world of aromatic herbs, exquisite spices, flavorful oils, and vinegars, as well as umami-rich and specialty ingredients, you open doors to a universe of flavors and possibilities. As you embark on your gourmet journey, remember that the quality and selection of your pantry ingredients play a pivotal role in the overall success of your dishes. So, stock your pantry with care, embrace the allure of exotic treasures, and let your gourmet creations shine with the essence of these essential ingredients and seasonings.

Chapter 3

From Amuse-Bouche to Grand Entrées: Creating Stunning Appetizers

Appetizers are the tantalizing prelude to a gourmet meal, setting the stage for an extraordinary dining experience. In this chapter, we explore the art of crafting stunning appetizers that awaken the senses and leave a lasting impression on your guests. From delicate amuse-bouche to elegant small plates, learn the techniques, flavor combinations, and presentation styles that elevate these miniature masterpieces to culinary works of art.

Amuse-Bouche: A bite-sized delight
Amuse-bouche, meaning "mouth amuser" in French, are tiny bites that tease the palate and awaken the taste buds. Discover the art of creating these delectable pre-meal treats, designed to excite the senses and set the tone for the dining experience. Learn about flavor contrasts, textural elements, and innovative presentations that showcase the essence of gourmet cuisine in a single, tantalizing morsel.

Canapés and Crostini: Small bites with big flavors
Canapés and crostini are elegant finger foods that make a statement at any gathering. Explore the world of creative toppings and spreads, from smoked salmon and herbed cream cheese on a crispy baguette slice to fig and prosciutto with balsamic reduction on toasted bread. Master the art of balancing flavors and textures to create bite-sized creations that leave a lasting impression on your guests.

Dumplings and Dim Sum: Steamed delights
Dumplings and dim sum offer a delightful fusion of flavors and textures, wrapped in delicate dough. Learn the

techniques behind crafting perfectly pleated dumplings, whether filled with succulent meats, seafood, or vibrant vegetables. Discover the art of steaming, frying, and pairing these little parcels with delectable dipping sauces, showcasing the diversity of Asian-inspired appetizers.

Tartlets and Quiches: Savory pastry wonders
Tartlets and quiches are savory delights encased in buttery pastry shells. Explore the art of making crisp tartlet shells and creamy quiche fillings, using a variety of ingredients like caramelized onions, gruyère cheese, and seasonal vegetables. Learn the principles of blind baking and the art of garnishing these miniature pastry wonders to create visually stunning appetizers.

Ceviche and Crudo: Refreshing seafood bites
Ceviche and crudo offer a refreshing and light option for seafood lovers. Dive into the world of marinating raw fish or seafood in citrus juices, infusing them with vibrant flavors. Discover the art of balancing acidity and adding complementary ingredients like fresh herbs, chilies, and fruits to create complex taste profiles. Master the techniques of slicing and plating these delicate appetizers to highlight the natural beauty of the seafood.

Bruschetta and Crostini: Bursting with freshness
Bruschetta and crostini are simple yet elegant appetizers that celebrate the freshness of seasonal ingredients. Explore the art of topping toasted bread with vibrant combinations such as ripe tomatoes, fresh basil, and drizzles of balsamic reduction. Experiment with variations using ingredients like creamy burrata cheese, roasted vegetables, or marinated olives. Learn to balance the flavors and textures to create irresistible bites of culinary bliss.

Gourmet Skewers: Creative presentations on a stick

Gourmet skewers are not only visually appealing but also offer a convenient way to enjoy flavorful bites. Master the art of assembling skewers with a combination of proteins, vegetables, and fruits, creating a harmonious blend of flavors and textures. Experiment with marinades, glazes, and rubs to infuse the ingredients with a burst of taste. Learn about innovative presentations and garnishes that elevate these skewered delights to a new level of sophistication.

Conclusion:
Crafting stunning appetizers is an art form that allows you to showcase your creativity and culinary expertise. From the delicate bites of amuse-bouche to the bold flavors of ceviche, each appetizer presents an opportunity to captivate your guests' taste buds and leave them eager for what's to come. By mastering the techniques, flavor combinations, and presentation styles explored in this chapter, you can create a remarkable prelude to your gourmet feast, setting the stage for an unforgettable dining experience. So, let your imagination soar, experiment with unique ingredients, and embark on the journey of creating stunning appetizers that will delight and amaze your guests.

Chapter 4

Soups and Bisques: A Symphony of Flavors

Soups and bisques are culinary symphonies that comfort the soul and excite the palate. In this chapter, we delve into the world of hearty soups and velvety bisques, exploring the techniques, flavor profiles, and garnishing styles that transform humble ingredients into bowls of culinary perfection. From creamy bisques to brothy soups, learn the art of creating harmonious flavor combinations and mastering the textures that make each spoonful a delight.

Classic Broths: Building a solid foundation

Broths form the backbone of many soups and bisques, infusing them with depth and richness. Explore the art of creating flavorful chicken, beef, and vegetable broths from scratch. Learn about the importance of simmering times, ingredient selection, and seasoning to achieve a well-balanced base. Discover how to transform simple broths into delicious consommés, adding clarity and elegance to your soup creations.

Creamy Bisques: Luxurious indulgence

Bisques are velvety, indulgent soups that showcase the richness of ingredients like shellfish, vegetables, or mushrooms. Dive into the art of creating luscious bisques, whether it's a classic lobster bisque or a roasted butternut squash bisque. Learn the techniques of simmering, pureeing, and straining to achieve a smooth and luxurious texture. Discover the magic of enhancing flavors with cream, aromatic spices, and a hint of acidity.

Vegetable Soups: Vibrant and nourishing

Vegetable soups offer a canvas for creativity, celebrating the bounty of seasonal produce. Explore the world of vibrant flavors and textures as you craft soups with roasted tomatoes, silky pumpkin, or hearty root vegetables. Learn how to balance the natural sweetness of vegetables with aromatic herbs, spices, and umami-rich ingredients. Discover the art of garnishing vegetable soups with fresh herbs, crispy croutons, or swirls of tangy yogurt.

Seafood Soups: Coastal delights
Seafood soups transport us to coastal regions, capturing the essence of the ocean in each spoonful. Delve into the creation of seafood chowders, bouillabaisse, or cioppino, rich with the flavors of fresh fish, succulent shellfish, and aromatic herbs. Learn the art of layering flavors, balancing the delicate sweetness of seafood with robust broths and aromatic ingredients. Master the techniques of shelling seafood and garnishing these soups with a touch of elegance.

Hearty Meat Soups: Comfort in a bowl
Hearty meat soups warm the soul and nourish the body with their robust flavors and comforting textures. Explore the art of creating beef stews, lamb tagines, or chicken noodle soups. Learn the techniques of slow cooking, braising, or pressure cooking to tenderize meats and infuse the broths with rich flavors. Discover the art of incorporating root vegetables, grains, and aromatic spices to create soul-satisfying bowls of comfort.

Cold Soups: Refreshing and innovative
Cold soups offer a refreshing twist, perfect for warm weather or as appetizers. Experiment with chilled gazpachos, creamy vichyssoises, or refreshing fruit soups. Learn the art of balancing flavors and textures in these chilled creations, incorporating ingredients like ripe tomatoes, cucumbers, melons, or avocados. Discover the art of garnishing cold

soups with herb-infused oils, vibrant microgreens, or a drizzle of aged balsamic vinegar.

Global Flavors: Journey through international soups
Gourmet cuisine knows no borders, and soups offer a passport to flavors from around the world. Embark on a culinary journey as you explore the aromatic spices of Moroccan harira, the tangy-sour notes of Vietnamese pho, or the complex flavors of Indian mulligatawny. Learn about traditional techniques, ingredient combinations, and garnishing styles that bring the authentic tastes of these international soups to your table.

Conclusion:
Soups and bisques are a symphony of flavors, showcasing the versatility and artistry of gourmet cuisine. From the comforting warmth of hearty meat soups to the velvety indulgence of creamy bisques, each bowl tells a story and invites us to savor the complexities of taste and texture. By mastering the techniques and exploring the diverse flavors presented in this chapter, you can create soups and bisques that transcend ordinary fare and become exceptional culinary experiences. So, let your creativity soar, embrace the beauty of seasonal ingredients, and compose your own symphony of flavors in every spoonful of these delectable creations.

Chapter 5

Exquisite Seafood Delights: Unleashing the Ocean's Bounty

The ocean offers a bountiful array of treasures, and seafood is a crown jewel of gourmet cuisine. In this chapter, we embark on a journey through the world of exquisite seafood delights, exploring the flavors, techniques, and culinary artistry that elevate these oceanic treasures to new heights. From delicate fish fillets to succulent shellfish, learn how to unleash the full potential of seafood and create extraordinary dishes that transport your taste buds to coastal paradise.

Perfectly Cooked Fish: A delicate balance
Cooking fish to perfection requires finesse and an understanding of its delicate nature. Explore the art of selecting and handling fish, from tender fillets to whole fish. Learn the techniques of pan-searing, grilling, and oven-roasting to achieve moist and flaky textures. Discover the importance of proper seasoning and flavor pairings that complement the natural sweetness of fish, elevating it to gourmet excellence.

Shellfish Spectacular: Briny treasures
Shellfish offer a spectrum of flavors, from the sweet succulence of lobster and crab to the briny richness of oysters and clams. Delve into the world of shellfish preparations, from steaming and grilling to poaching and sautéing. Learn the art of shucking oysters, cracking crab legs, and deveining shrimp. Discover the perfect balance of flavors in sauces and accompaniments that enhance the natural taste of these briny treasures.

Ceviche and Tartare: The essence of freshness

Ceviche and tartare showcase the raw beauty of seafood, celebrating its freshness and delicate flavors. Dive into the art of marinating raw fish or shellfish in citrus juices, infusing them with vibrant flavors. Learn the techniques of dicing, mincing, and seasoning seafood to create exquisite tartare. Discover the art of balancing acidity, heat, and freshness to create refreshing and tantalizing bites of culinary delight.

Seafood Paella and Risotto: Rice masterpieces
Paella and risotto are culinary masterpieces that showcase the harmony of seafood and rice. Explore the techniques of creating rich and flavorful seafood paellas, whether it's the classic Valencian version or regional variations with unique ingredients. Learn the art of making creamy and perfectly cooked risottos, incorporating seafood like shrimp, scallops, or squid. Discover the secrets of layering flavors and achieving the ideal texture in these rice-based delicacies.

Grilled and Smoked Seafood: Fire and flavor
Grilling and smoking techniques add a touch of smoky char and complexity to seafood. Explore the art of grilling whole fish, shrimp skewers, or scallops, infusing them with the essence of fire. Learn about different types of wood for smoking and how they impart distinct flavors to salmon, trout, or oysters. Discover the balance between heat and time to achieve tender and smoky seafood creations.

Seafood Pasta: Elegant and indulgent
Seafood and pasta come together in perfect harmony, creating elegant and indulgent dishes. Delve into the world of seafood pastas, from delicate linguine alle vongole (clam pasta) to rich lobster ravioli. Learn the art of cooking pasta al dente and creating flavorful seafood sauces. Discover the importance of balancing the richness of seafood with vibrant herbs, citrus zests, and a hint of spice.

Sushi and Sashimi: The art of precision
Sushi and sashimi are epitomes of precision and simplicity, allowing the pure flavors of seafood to shine. Explore the art of preparing sushi rice, slicing sashimi-grade fish, and assembling nigiri or maki rolls. Learn about the different types of sushi, from classic favorites like tuna and salmon to adventurous creations with uni (sea urchin) or eel. Discover the elegance of garnishes and dipping sauces that complement the pristine flavors of sushi and sashimi.

Conclusion:
Seafood is a gift from the ocean, offering a vast array of flavors, textures, and culinary possibilities. By mastering the techniques and exploring the diverse range of seafood delights presented in this chapter, you can unlock the full potential of these oceanic treasures. From perfectly cooked fish to shellfish spectacles, ceviche and tartare to grilled and smoked creations, seafood pasta to sushi and sashimi, let your culinary imagination soar as you unleash the ocean's bounty and create exquisite seafood dishes that will delight and amaze your guests. Embrace the flavors of the sea and embark on a gastronomic journey that celebrates the wonders of seafood in all its glory.

Chapter 6

The Art of Meat: Mastering Gourmet Meat Cookery

Meat is the epitome of indulgence in gourmet cuisine, with its rich flavors and succulent textures. In this chapter, we dive into the art of meat cookery, exploring the techniques, cuts, and flavor profiles that transform ordinary meats into extraordinary culinary experiences. From tender steaks to slow-cooked roasts, learn the secrets of mastering gourmet meat cookery and delighting your taste buds with each savory bite.

Steak Perfection: From rare to well-done
Steak is the crown jewel of meat cookery, and achieving the perfect doneness requires precision and skill. Explore the different cuts of steak, from tender filet mignon to juicy ribeye. Learn the techniques of searing, grilling, and sous vide cooking to achieve your desired level of doneness, whether it's a rare, medium-rare, or well-done steak. Discover the art of seasoning and resting meat to enhance its flavors and ensure optimal tenderness.

Braising and Stewing: Tender and flavorful
Braising and stewing methods transform tough cuts of meat into meltingly tender and flavorful dishes. Delve into the art of braising short ribs, osso buco, or lamb shanks, creating succulent dishes that are infused with aromatic flavors. Learn the techniques of searing, deglazing, and slow cooking to achieve tender meat and rich, concentrated sauces. Discover the perfect balance of seasonings and accompaniments that elevate these hearty dishes to gourmet status.

Roasting and Glazing: The art of caramelization

Roasting is a timeless cooking method that brings out the natural flavors of meat while creating a beautiful caramelized crust. Explore the techniques of roasting whole chickens, racks of lamb, or pork tenderloins to juicy perfection. Learn the art of creating flavorful glazes and marinades that enhance the meat's natural sweetness and create a stunning presentation. Discover the importance of resting and carving meat to retain its moisture and tenderness.

Grilling and Barbecuing: Flames and smoky goodness
Grilling and barbecuing methods infuse meat with smoky flavors and create a mouthwatering charred exterior. Dive into the art of grilling thick-cut steaks, tender chicken breasts, or juicy burgers, achieving those coveted grill marks and smoky flavors. Learn about different types of wood and charcoal for barbecuing, and how they impart distinct aromas and flavors to ribs, brisket, or pulled pork. Discover the secrets of marinades, rubs, and sauces that elevate grilled and barbecued meats to new heights of deliciousness.

Sous Vide: Precision cooking
Sous vide is a technique that involves cooking meat in a precise temperature-controlled water bath, resulting in incredibly tender and evenly cooked meat. Explore the world of sous vide cooking, from perfectly cooked steaks to tender pork chops or chicken breasts. Learn the science behind sous vide and how to season and vacuum-seal meat for optimal results. Discover the art of searing meat post-sous vide to add a caramelized crust and enhance the visual appeal.

Charcuterie and Dry Aging: The art of preservation
Charcuterie and dry aging are methods of preserving and enhancing the flavors of meat. Delve into the world of artisanal cured meats, from prosciutto and salami to terrines and pâtés. Learn the techniques of curing, smoking, and fermenting to create a variety of charcuterie delights.

Discover the process of dry aging beef to intensify its flavors and achieve exceptional tenderness. Explore the art of assembling beautiful charcuterie boards, showcasing an array of flavors and textures.

Global Inspirations: Exploring meat in international cuisine
Meat holds a prominent place in cuisines around the world, each offering unique flavors and cooking techniques. Embark on a culinary journey as you explore the spicy curries of India, the tender kebabs of the Middle East, the savory stews of France, or the hearty barbecue traditions of the United States. Learn about the different cuts, spices, and marination styles that contribute to the distinctiveness of meat dishes in various global cuisines.

Conclusion:
Mastering the art of meat cookery is a journey of flavors, textures, and techniques. From achieving steak perfection to creating tender braised dishes, from roasting with precision to infusing smoky goodness through grilling and barbecuing, each method offers a unique experience for meat lovers. By exploring the techniques and flavor profiles presented in this chapter, you can elevate your meat cookery skills to gourmet levels, delighting your palate with succulent bites and savoring the indulgence that only well-prepared meat can provide. So, embrace the artistry of meat cookery, experiment with cuts, flavors, and techniques, and let your culinary prowess shine as you create memorable gourmet meat dishes that will leave a lasting impression on your guests.

Chapter 7

Poultry Perfection: Elevating Chicken, Duck, and Game Birds

Poultry, with its tender meat and versatile flavors, offers endless possibilities for gourmet culinary creations. In this chapter, we delve into the world of poultry, exploring the techniques, flavors, and cooking methods that elevate chicken, duck, and game birds to new heights of perfection. From succulent roasted chicken to rich and tender duck confit, learn the art of poultry cookery and discover the secrets to creating exquisite dishes that will delight your palate.

The Classic Roast Chicken: Simple yet sublime
The classic roast chicken is a testament to the beauty of simplicity. Learn the art of selecting the perfect chicken, seasoning it to perfection, and achieving a crispy golden skin and juicy meat. Discover the importance of proper trussing and resting techniques to ensure an evenly cooked bird. Explore various flavor variations, from herb-infused roast chicken to citrus and spice-rubbed versions, that add depth and complexity to this timeless dish.

Duck Delights: From confit to crispy skin
Duck is known for its rich and distinctive flavors, and mastering the art of duck cookery opens up a world of indulgence. Explore the techniques of preparing duck confit, a slow-cooked method that renders the meat tender and flavorful. Learn the art of crisping the duck skin to perfection, creating a crackling crust that contrasts with the succulent meat. Discover the interplay of flavors, from sweet and fruity sauces to tangy glazes, that elevate duck dishes to gourmet status.

Game Birds: A wild and flavorful experience
Game birds, such as quail, pheasant, and partridge, offer a unique and robust flavor profile. Delve into the world of game bird cookery, learning the techniques to handle and prepare these smaller and more delicate birds. Explore the art of pan-searing, roasting, or grilling game birds to perfection, creating dishes that showcase their natural flavors. Discover the perfect balance of herbs, spices, and complementary ingredients that enhance the wild and gamey essence of these birds.

Chicken and Duck Confit: Tender and flavorful
Confit is a traditional French cooking technique that involves slowly cooking meat in its own fat, resulting in incredibly tender and flavorful results. Learn the art of preparing chicken and duck confit, infusing the meat with rich and savory flavors. Discover the techniques of curing, slow cooking, and storing the confit for optimal results. Explore creative ways to incorporate confit into other dishes, such as salads, pastas, or sandwiches, to add a luxurious touch to your culinary repertoire.

Poultry Roulades and Stuffed Creations: Elegance and creativity
Roulades and stuffed poultry dishes showcase the elegance and creativity of gourmet cuisine. Learn the techniques of butterflying and pounding chicken breasts or duck breasts to create flat surfaces for stuffing. Explore a variety of fillings, from flavorful herb and cheese combinations to indulgent foie gras or mushroom duxelles. Discover the art of rolling, tying, and searing roulades to achieve even cooking and maximize flavor infusion. Unleash your culinary creativity as you experiment with different stuffing ingredients and presentation styles.

International Inspirations: Global poultry flavors
Poultry dishes vary widely across different cuisines, offering a plethora of flavor profiles and culinary traditions. Explore the aromatic spices of Indian tandoori chicken, the succulent rotisserie chickens of Latin America, or the fragrant duck dishes of Chinese cuisine. Learn about the unique marinades, spice blends, and cooking techniques that contribute to the distinctiveness of poultry dishes in various cultures. Let the flavors of the world inspire your poultry creations, taking your taste buds on a global journey of culinary delights.

Sous Vide Poultry: Tenderness to perfection
Sous vide cooking is a precise and gentle method that ensures poultry is cooked to tender perfection. Dive into the world of sous vide poultry, from succulent chicken breasts to tender duck breasts. Learn the art of seasoning, vacuum-sealing, and temperature control to achieve the desired level of doneness and retain maximum juiciness. Discover the finishing techniques, such as searing or crisping the skin, that elevate sous vide poultry to a whole new level of culinary excellence.

Conclusion:
Poultry is a canvas for gourmet creativity, offering tender meat and a wide range of flavors. By mastering the techniques and exploring the flavors presented in this chapter, you can elevate your poultry cookery skills to new heights. From the simplicity of a perfectly roasted chicken to the indulgence of duck confit or the robust flavors of game birds, let your culinary imagination soar. Embrace the versatility of poultry and create exquisite dishes that will captivate your palate and impress your guests. Poultry perfection awaits, and with the knowledge and techniques learned here, you can achieve it with confidence and flair.

Chapter 8

Sensational Sauces: Elevating Flavors to New Heights

Sauces are the crown jewels of gourmet cuisine, adding depth, complexity, and a burst of flavor to any dish. In this chapter, we delve into the art of creating sensational sauces that elevate the taste of your culinary creations to new heights. From velvety reductions to creamy emulsions, learn the techniques, ingredients, and flavor combinations that will transform your dishes into unforgettable culinary experiences.

The Fundamentals of Sauce Making: Building Blocks of Flavor
Mastering the fundamentals of sauce making is essential for any aspiring gourmet chef. Explore the techniques of creating flavorful stocks, reducing liquids to intensify flavors, and thickening agents to achieve the perfect consistency. Learn about the classic French mother sauces and their variations, such as velouté, béchamel, and hollandaise, as well as the principles of balancing flavors and adjusting seasoning. Develop a strong foundation in sauce making that will serve as a basis for creating your own unique and sensational sauces.

Reduction Sauces: Concentrated Elegance
Reduction sauces are all about concentrating flavors and creating rich, intense, and velvety sauces. Delve into the art of reducing liquids, such as wine, vinegar, or stocks, to create a base for your sauces. Learn the techniques of deglazing, incorporating aromatics, and adding finishing touches, such as butter or herbs, to enhance the depth of flavor. Explore a variety of reduction sauces, from classic red wine reductions

to tangy balsamic glazes, that will elevate your dishes to a new level of sophistication.

Emulsion Sauces: Creamy and Luxurious

Emulsion sauces are creamy, luxurious, and decadent, adding a velvety texture and a burst of flavor to any dish. Explore the techniques of emulsifying oil and liquid ingredients, such as egg yolks or vinegar, to create luscious sauces like mayonnaise, hollandaise, or aioli. Learn the art of tempering, balancing acidity, and incorporating additional flavors, such as herbs or spices, to enhance the overall taste. Discover the versatility of emulsion sauces and how they can transform simple ingredients into extraordinary culinary creations.

Cream and Butter Sauces: Indulgence on the Palate

Cream and butter sauces are synonymous with indulgence, adding richness, smoothness, and a velvety mouthfeel to dishes. Delve into the techniques of incorporating cream, butter, or both into your sauces to create a luxurious texture and enhance flavors. Learn the art of reducing, simmering, or whisking to achieve the perfect consistency and avoid curdling. Explore a range of cream and butter sauces, from classic béarnaise to velvety mushroom cream sauces, that will elevate your dishes to gourmet status.

Infused and Herb Sauces: A Symphony of Aromatics

Infused and herb sauces are all about infusing flavors and aromatics into your culinary creations. Learn the art of steeping herbs, spices, or other ingredients in liquids, such as oils or vinegars, to create delicate and fragrant sauces. Discover the techniques of balancing flavors, straining, and incorporating additional elements, such as citrus zest or garlic, to enhance the overall taste. Explore a variety of infused and herb sauces, from aromatic basil pesto to zesty lemon-infused vinaigrette, that will bring a symphony of flavors to your dishes.

Global Inspirations: Exploring Flavors from Around the World
Sauces play a vital role in cuisines from around the world, each offering its own unique flavors and techniques. Embark on a culinary journey as you explore the spicy salsas of Mexico, the tangy chimichurri of Argentina, the piquant curry sauces of India, or the fragrant soy-based sauces of East Asia. Learn about the key ingredients, spices, and cooking methods that contribute to the distinctiveness of sauces in various global cuisines. Let the flavors of the world inspire your sauce creations and bring a global flair to your gourmet dishes.

Conclusion:
Sauces are the magic that transforms a dish from ordinary to extraordinary, adding layers of flavor, texture, and visual appeal. By mastering the techniques and principles presented in this chapter, you can elevate your sauce-making skills to new heights. From reduction sauces that intensify flavors to creamy emulsions that add a luxurious touch, let your creativity flow as you experiment with flavors, ingredients, and techniques. Embrace the art of sauce making, balance flavors with precision, and watch as your dishes come alive with sensational flavors that will impress and delight your guests. With a repertoire of sensational sauces at your disposal, your gourmet culinary journey reaches new heights of culinary excellence.

Chapter 9

Decadent Pasta Creations: Fresh, Homemade, and Gourmet

Pasta is a beloved staple in cuisines around the world, and there's nothing quite like the taste and texture of fresh, homemade pasta. In this chapter, we dive into the art of creating decadent pasta creations that will transport you to the streets of Italy and beyond. From delicate filled pastas to hearty and satisfying sauces, learn the techniques, tips, and flavor combinations that will elevate your pasta dishes to gourmet status.

The Magic of Fresh Pasta: From Dough to Delight
Fresh pasta is the epitome of culinary craftsmanship, and there's a certain joy in creating pasta from scratch. Discover the techniques of making fresh pasta dough, from the traditional egg-based varieties to specialty flours and gluten-free options. Learn the art of kneading, resting, and rolling out the dough to achieve the perfect thickness and texture. Explore the various pasta shapes, from silky tagliatelle to delicate ravioli, and let your creativity shine as you experiment with flavors and fillings.

Stuffed Pasta Delights: From Ravioli to Tortellini
Stuffed pastas are a true indulgence, offering a burst of flavor with every bite. Delve into the art of creating stuffed pasta delights, such as ravioli, tortellini, or agnolotti. Learn the techniques of rolling out the pasta dough, filling it with a variety of ingredients, and sealing it to create perfect parcels of deliciousness. Explore a range of fillings, from classic combinations like ricotta and spinach to more adventurous flavors like lobster and saffron. Discover the art of pairing

stuffed pastas with complementary sauces that enhance their flavors and textures.

The Perfect Pasta Sauces: A Symphony of Flavors
Sauces are the soul of pasta dishes, and mastering the art of sauce-making is essential for creating gourmet creations. Explore a variety of pasta sauces, from classic marinara and creamy Alfredo to rich Bolognese and vibrant pesto. Learn the techniques of balancing flavors, simmering, reducing, and incorporating additional ingredients to create complex and harmonious flavors. Discover the art of matching the right sauce with the perfect pasta shape to create an unforgettable culinary experience.

Seafood Pasta Extravaganza: A Marriage Made in Heaven
The combination of seafood and pasta is a match made in culinary heaven, offering a symphony of flavors from the sea. Dive into the world of seafood pasta extravaganza as you explore the techniques of cooking seafood to perfection, whether it's succulent shrimp, tender scallops, or delicate lobster. Learn the art of pairing seafood with complementary pasta shapes and sauces, such as linguine with white wine and clam sauce or spaghetti with garlic, chili, and prawns. Discover the nuances of balancing flavors and textures to create sensational seafood pasta dishes that will transport you to coastal regions around the world.

Vegetarian Pasta Delights: From Garden to Plate
Vegetarian pasta dishes showcase the vibrant flavors of fresh vegetables and herbs, offering a delightful and wholesome culinary experience. Explore the techniques of incorporating seasonal vegetables, such as roasted tomatoes, sautéed mushrooms, or grilled zucchini, into your pasta creations. Learn the art of enhancing vegetarian dishes with flavorful herbs, aromatic spices, and quality cheeses. Discover the joy

of creating vegetarian pasta sauces, from creamy spinach and ricotta to tangy roasted vegetable medleys, that will satisfy even the most discerning palates.

Pasta with a Twist: Fusion and International Inspirations
Pasta is a versatile canvas for culinary creativity, allowing you to infuse it with flavors from different cuisines around the world. Explore the fusion and international inspirations of pasta dishes, such as Thai-inspired peanut noodles, Mexican-inspired pasta with chipotle sauce, or Indian-inspired curried pasta. Learn about the key ingredients, spices, and cooking techniques that contribute to the distinctiveness of these fusion creations. Let your taste buds travel the globe as you experiment with unique flavor combinations and create pasta dishes that marry different culinary traditions.

Conclusion:
Fresh, homemade pasta is a labor of love that results in sublime culinary experiences. With the techniques and tips presented in this chapter, you can elevate your pasta creations to gourmet heights. From mastering the art of fresh pasta dough to crafting delectable stuffed pastas, experimenting with flavorful sauces, and exploring seafood, vegetarian, and fusion inspirations, your pasta repertoire will know no bounds. Embrace the joy of pasta-making and let your culinary creativity shine as you create decadent pasta creations that will delight your senses and impress your guests. Prepare to embark on a journey of taste and texture as you savor the indulgent and gourmet world of homemade pasta.

Chapter 10

Vegetarian Gastronomy: Celebrating the Bounty of Nature

Vegetarian cuisine is not just a culinary choice; it's a celebration of the bountiful flavors, textures, and colors that nature has to offer. In this chapter, we delve into the world of vegetarian gastronomy, exploring the diverse and exciting possibilities of plant-based cooking. From vibrant salads to hearty mains, learn the techniques, ingredients, and creative combinations that will elevate vegetarian dishes to gourmet status.

The Vegetarian Pantry: Staples for Flavorful Creations
Building a well-stocked vegetarian pantry is essential for creating delicious and satisfying meat-free meals. Discover the key ingredients that form the foundation of vegetarian gastronomy, such as legumes, grains, nuts, and seeds. Learn about the importance of flavor enhancers like nutritional yeast, miso, and tamari, as well as a variety of herbs and spices that add depth and complexity to vegetarian dishes. Unlock the secrets of combining ingredients to create flavorful vegetarian bases, sauces, and dressings that will form the backbone of your culinary creations.

Salads that Satisfy: From Simple to Spectacular
Salads are not just a side dish; they can be the star of a vegetarian gastronomic experience. Explore the art of creating salads that satisfy both in taste and presentation. Learn the techniques of balancing flavors, textures, and colors to create vibrant and enticing salads. From simple green salads with tangy vinaigrettes to hearty grain salads with roasted vegetables and creamy dressings, discover the

limitless possibilities of vegetarian salads and let your creativity shine.

Creative Vegetable Preparations: From Roasting to Grilling

Vegetables are versatile ingredients that can be prepared in countless ways, each offering its own unique flavors and textures. Delve into the techniques of roasting, grilling, sautéing, and braising vegetables to bring out their natural sweetness and enhance their flavors. Learn the art of caramelization, charred edges, and perfectly cooked textures that transform vegetables into culinary delights. Explore a variety of vegetable preparations, from roasted root vegetables with balsamic glaze to grilled eggplant with tahini sauce, and elevate your vegetarian dishes to gourmet levels.

Plant-Based Protein Power: Legumes, Tofu, and Beyond

Vegetarian gastronomy offers a wealth of plant-based protein sources that can rival their meat counterparts in flavor and nutrition. Discover the world of legumes, such as lentils, chickpeas, and black beans, and learn how to incorporate them into hearty and satisfying vegetarian dishes. Explore the versatility of tofu and tempeh, and master the art of marinating, grilling, and braising these plant-based proteins for maximum flavor and texture. Unleash the potential of plant-based proteins and create vegetarian mains that will satisfy even the most discerning palates.

The Art of Vegetable Dishes: Starring the Season's Best

Vegetables are the shining stars of vegetarian gastronomy, and celebrating the season's best produce is a testament to the flavors and freshness that nature provides. Learn the art of showcasing vegetables in their purest form, whether it's a simple roasted beet salad or a complex ratatouille. Discover the techniques of layering flavors, incorporating herbs and spices, and creating visually stunning vegetable dishes that will impress and delight. Embrace the diversity of vegetables and let their natural flavors take center stage in your vegetarian gastronomic creations.

Global Vegetarian Inspirations: Flavors from Around the World
Vegetarian cuisine knows no boundaries, drawing inspiration from various cultures and cuisines around the world. Embark on a culinary journey as you explore global vegetarian inspirations, from Indian curries bursting with aromatic spices to Middle Eastern mezze platters filled with vibrant flavors. Learn about the unique ingredients, cooking techniques, and flavor combinations that contribute to the distinctiveness of vegetarian dishes in different cultures. Let the global vegetarian inspirations ignite your creativity and bring a world of flavors to your gourmet vegetarian repertoire.

Conclusion:
Vegetarian gastronomy is a celebration of the incredible flavors, textures, and colors that plant-based ingredients offer. By exploring the techniques, ingredients, and creative combinations presented in this chapter, you can elevate vegetarian dishes to gourmet levels. From building a well-stocked vegetarian pantry to creating satisfying salads, mastering vegetable preparations, incorporating plant-based proteins, and drawing inspiration from global cuisines, the world of vegetarian gastronomy becomes an exciting and fulfilling culinary adventure. Embrace the bounty of nature, celebrate the vibrant flavors of vegetables, and let your creativity soar as you create gourmet vegetarian dishes that will delight both vegetarians and meat-eaters alike. Prepare to be amazed as you discover the endless possibilities of vegetarian cuisine and embark on a journey of culinary excellence.

Chapter 11

Gourmet Grains and Legumes: Elevating Simple Staples

Grains and legumes are humble staples that have been a part of human diets for centuries. In this chapter, we explore the art of transforming these simple ingredients into gourmet culinary creations. From hearty grain-based dishes to flavorful legume-centric recipes, we delve into the techniques, flavors, and creative combinations that elevate grains and legumes to new heights of gastronomic delight.

The World of Grains: Exploring Diversity and Flavor
Grains are the foundation of many cuisines around the world, offering a wide range of flavors, textures, and nutritional benefits. Discover the diverse world of grains, from familiar staples like rice and wheat to lesser-known varieties such as quinoa, farro, and millet. Learn about the characteristics of each grain and how to cook them to perfection, whether it's achieving fluffy rice or al dente quinoa. Explore the art of pairing grains with complementary flavors and ingredients to create gourmet grain-based dishes that will captivate your taste buds.

Risottos and Pilafs: The Art of Grain Cookery
Risottos and pilafs are timeless classics that showcase the versatility and richness of grains. Delve into the art of creating creamy and flavorful risottos, whether it's the traditional Italian mushroom risotto or a creative twist with seasonal vegetables and herbs. Learn the techniques of achieving the perfect consistency and marrying flavors in every spoonful. Explore the world of pilafs, from fragrant basmati rice with aromatic spices to hearty bulgur wheat with roasted vegetables, and discover the art of creating

harmonious grain-based dishes that will impress both family and guests.

Legume Love: Unleashing the Power of Protein
Legumes, including beans, lentils, and chickpeas, are nutritional powerhouses packed with protein, fiber, and essential nutrients. Dive into the world of legume-based dishes and explore the techniques that bring out their flavors and textures. Learn the art of cooking beans from scratch, from soaking and simmering to achieving tender yet intact beans. Discover the versatility of lentils, whether it's in a comforting lentil soup or a hearty lentil-based salad. Embrace the magic of chickpeas and explore their potential in dishes like hummus, falafel, and stews. Unleash the power of legumes and elevate your dishes with their nutty flavors and creamy textures.

Grain and Legume Combinations: A Marriage of Flavors and Textures
The combination of grains and legumes creates a harmonious union of flavors, textures, and nutritional benefits. Explore the art of pairing grains with legumes to create wholesome and satisfying meals. Learn about classic combinations like rice and beans in Latin American cuisine or lentils and bulgur in Middle Eastern cuisine. Discover creative combinations such as quinoa and black bean salads or barley and chickpea stews. Unleash your culinary creativity and let the synergy of grains and legumes elevate your dishes to gourmet levels.

Gourmet Grain Bowls: Wholesome and Flavorful Delights
Grain bowls have gained popularity in recent years for their simplicity, nutrition, and versatility. Delve into the world of gourmet grain bowls and learn the techniques of creating balanced and flavorful combinations. From quinoa and roasted vegetable bowls to barley and tofu stir-fry bowls,

explore the myriad of ingredients, sauces, and toppings that can transform a simple bowl of grains and legumes into a gourmet masterpiece. Discover the art of layering flavors and textures, and let the colors and freshness of the ingredients shine through.

Breads, Flatbreads, and Wraps: Grain-Based Delicacies
Grains are the foundation of many bread-based delicacies, and mastering the art of bread-making opens up a world of possibilities. Learn the techniques of creating artisanal breads, from rustic sourdough loaves to fluffy naan and tortillas. Explore the world of flatbreads and wraps, such as socca, dosa, and lavash, and discover their unique flavors and textures. Let the aroma of freshly baked bread fill your kitchen and unleash your creativity as you experiment with grain-based delicacies that will elevate any meal.

Conclusion:

Grains and legumes, once considered simple staples, have the power to create gourmet culinary experiences. By exploring the techniques, flavors, and creative combinations presented in this chapter, you can transform grains and legumes into extraordinary dishes that will delight your senses. From exploring the diverse world of grains to mastering the art of risottos and pilafs, unleashing the power of legumes, creating flavorful grain and legume combinations, and embracing the versatility of grain bowls and bread-based delicacies, you will discover the endless possibilities of gourmet grain and legume cuisine. Embrace these humble ingredients, celebrate their nutritional benefits, and let your culinary prowess shine as you create elevated dishes that showcase the beauty and flavors of grains and legumes. Prepare to embark on a gastronomic journey that will redefine the way you perceive these simple staples.

Chapter 12

Salads and Dressings: Innovative Combinations and Artful Presentations

Salads have evolved from simple side dishes to center-stage culinary delights. In this chapter, we dive into the world of salads and dressings, exploring innovative combinations of ingredients and artful presentations that will take your salad game to new heights. Discover the techniques, flavors, and creative approaches that will transform a bowl of greens into a masterpiece of taste, texture, and visual appeal.

The Art of Salad Composition: Balancing Flavors and Textures

Creating a well-balanced salad requires a keen understanding of flavors, textures, and ingredient combinations. Learn the art of composing salads that delight the palate and satisfy the senses. Explore the interplay of crispness, tenderness, sweetness, acidity, and umami as you experiment with various greens, vegetables, fruits, nuts, and cheeses. Discover the secrets of layering flavors and textures to create harmonious and dynamic salads that captivate the taste buds.

Beyond the Greens: Exploring Salad Foundations

While greens form the base of most salads, there are countless other ingredients that can serve as the foundation of a remarkable salad. Delve into the world of alternative salad foundations, such as grains, legumes, roasted vegetables, and even noodles. Learn how to combine these elements with finesse, creating salads that are both hearty and nutritious. From quinoa and roasted vegetable salads to lentil and feta grain bowls, explore the possibilities beyond traditional green salads.

From Simple to Spectacular: Dressings that Elevate
A well-crafted dressing can elevate a salad from good to extraordinary. Discover the art of making homemade dressings that burst with flavor and complement the ingredients in your salad. Master the techniques of emulsifying vinaigrettes, creating creamy dressings, and balancing acidity and sweetness. Experiment with a variety of ingredients, such as herbs, spices, citrus juices, vinegars, and oils, to craft dressings that are both versatile and unique. From classic vinaigrettes to tangy yogurt-based dressings, let your creativity flow as you elevate your salads with sensational dressings.

Creative Salad Combinations: Unexpected Pairings and Flavors
The world of salad combinations is vast and full of exciting possibilities. Explore unexpected pairings and flavors as you push the boundaries of traditional salad ingredients. Experiment with contrasting tastes and textures, combining ingredients like fruits and cheeses, nuts and seeds, or roasted vegetables and grains. Let your imagination run wild and create innovative salads that surprise and delight your taste buds. From a watermelon and feta salad with mint to a roasted beet and citrus salad with goat cheese, discover the joy of creating salads that are anything but ordinary.

Artful Presentations: Making Salads a Feast for the Eyes
Aesthetics play a crucial role in the enjoyment of a salad. Learn the art of artful presentations, turning your salads into visual feasts that stimulate the appetite. Explore different plating techniques, garnishes, and edible flowers to create visually stunning salads that are as beautiful as they are delicious. Master the art of balancing colors, shapes, and heights to create Instagram-worthy salads that impress both guests and family.

Salad as a Meal: Creating Satisfying and Nourishing Main Course Salads

Salads can be more than just a side dish; they can also serve as satisfying and nourishing main courses. Discover the techniques of creating substantial salads that incorporate proteins, whole grains, and hearty vegetables. Learn how to create balanced and filling main course salads that leave you feeling satisfied and nourished. From protein-packed salads with grilled chicken or seared tofu to grain-based salads with roasted vegetables and creamy dressings, explore the possibilities of creating salads that can stand alone as a complete meal.

Conclusion:

Salads have transformed from simple starters to culinary works of art. By exploring the techniques, flavors, and creative combinations presented in this chapter, you can elevate your salads to new heights of gastronomic pleasure. From mastering the art of salad composition and exploring alternative foundations to crafting sensational dressings and creating innovative combinations, the world of salads becomes a canvas for your culinary creativity. Embrace the beauty of salad presentations and discover the joy of creating visually stunning dishes that are as delightful to the eyes as they are to the palate. Prepare to embark on a salad adventure, where each bite offers a burst of flavors and textures that will leave you craving for more.

Chapter 13

The Art of Cheese: Pairing and Presenting Fine Cheeses

Cheese, with its wide range of flavors, textures, and aromas, is a culinary treasure that deserves to be celebrated. In this chapter, we delve into the art of cheese, exploring the nuances of different varieties, mastering the art of pairing, and learning how to present fine cheeses in an elegant and enticing manner. Whether you're a seasoned cheese connoisseur or a novice enthusiast, this chapter will guide you through the world of cheese, unlocking its potential to elevate your culinary experiences.

Cheese Appreciation: Exploring Varieties and Characteristics
To truly appreciate cheese, it's essential to understand the diverse range of varieties and their unique characteristics. Dive into the world of cheese, from soft and creamy Brie to sharp and tangy Cheddar, from nutty and complex Gouda to pungent and aromatic Blue cheeses. Learn about the different cheese families, including bloomy rind, washed rind, semi-soft, hard, and blue-veined cheeses. Explore the flavors, textures, and aging processes that contribute to the distinctiveness of each cheese, expanding your cheese knowledge and developing your palate.

The Art of Cheese Pairing: Creating Harmonious Combinations
Pairing cheese with complementary flavors and textures is an art form that can elevate the taste experience to new heights. Discover the principles of cheese pairing, exploring the interplay of sweet, salty, tangy, and savory elements. Learn how to create harmonious combinations by considering the

cheese's characteristics, such as its acidity, creaminess, and intensity. Experiment with pairing cheese with fruits, nuts, honey, cured meats, crackers, and bread, discovering the magic that unfolds when the right flavors come together. Unlock the secrets of cheese pairing and create memorable taste experiences that showcase the best of each cheese.

Building the Perfect Cheese Board: A Feast for the Senses
A well-curated cheese board is a feast for the senses, offering a variety of flavors, textures, and visual appeal. Explore the art of building the perfect cheese board, selecting a diverse range of cheeses that offer contrasting tastes and textures. Learn how to create a balance of flavors, from mild and creamy cheeses to bold and robust options. Consider the inclusion of different cheese families, as well as a variety of accompaniments, such as fresh and dried fruits, artisanal crackers, crusty bread, nuts, olives, and spreads. Master the art of arranging the cheeses and accompaniments in an aesthetically pleasing manner, creating a cheese board that entices both the eyes and the taste buds.

The Cheese Course: A Culinary Journey
In many cultures, the cheese course is an essential part of a formal meal, offering a transition from the main course to dessert. Learn about the traditions and etiquettes surrounding the cheese course, and discover the joy of creating a culinary journey for your guests. Explore the art of selecting a curated selection of cheeses that tell a story, from local favorites to internationally renowned classics. Consider the progression of flavors, textures, and intensities, ensuring a memorable experience for each guest. Learn the techniques of serving and cutting cheese, and savor the moments as your guests indulge in a sensory exploration of fine cheeses.

Cooking with Cheese: From Classic to Creative

Cheese isn't just meant for platters and pairings; it's also a versatile ingredient in the kitchen. Delve into the world of cooking with cheese, from classic dishes like fondue, quiches, and gratins to more creative endeavors like stuffed pastas, cheese-infused sauces, and gourmet grilled cheeses. Discover the techniques of melting, melting, and incorporating cheese into recipes, enhancing flavors and adding a creamy richness to your dishes. Experiment with different varieties of cheese and let your culinary creativity shine as you explore the endless possibilities of cooking with cheese.

Conclusion:
Cheese, with its multitude of flavors, textures, and aromas, is a culinary treasure that deserves to be celebrated. By delving into the art of cheese, from understanding its varieties and characteristics to mastering the art of pairing and presenting, you can unlock the true potential of this versatile ingredient. Whether enjoyed on its own, paired with complementary flavors, or incorporated into recipes, cheese has the power to elevate your culinary experiences and create moments of pure gastronomic delight. Embrace the art of cheese and embark on a journey that will satisfy both your palate and your passion for exquisite flavors.

Chapter 14

From Farm to Table: Embracing Locally Sourced Ingredients

In recent years, the farm-to-table movement has gained popularity as people increasingly recognize the importance of supporting local farmers and consuming fresh, seasonal ingredients. In this chapter, we explore the concept of embracing locally sourced ingredients and the benefits it brings to your gourmet cooking. From understanding the advantages of eating locally to discovering ways to incorporate these ingredients into your recipes, this chapter will inspire you to forge a stronger connection between the food on your plate and the farms in your community.

The Importance of Locally Sourced Ingredients: Freshness, Flavor, and Sustainability
Locally sourced ingredients offer numerous benefits that go beyond the typical grocery store fare. Discover the importance of eating locally and supporting small-scale farmers. Explore how locally sourced ingredients are typically fresher, as they don't have to travel long distances to reach your plate. Learn about the impact on flavor and nutritional value when ingredients are picked at their peak ripeness. Dive into the sustainability aspect of local sourcing, reducing carbon footprint and supporting a more resilient and diverse food system. Embrace the notion of knowing where your food comes from and the positive impact it can have on both your health and the environment.

Building Relationships with Local Farmers and Producers
Connecting with local farmers and producers is a wonderful way to embrace locally sourced ingredients. Discover the joy

of visiting farmers' markets, where you can meet the people behind the food, learn about their practices, and develop relationships based on trust and shared values. Explore the possibilities of joining community-supported agriculture (CSA) programs, where you receive a weekly share of fresh produce directly from local farms. Engage in conversations with farmers and producers, ask questions, and gain a deeper understanding of their farming methods, seasonal offerings, and the stories behind the food. Building relationships with local food producers not only enhances your connection to the ingredients but also contributes to a vibrant and resilient local food community.

Seasonal Eating: Celebrating the Flavors of Each Season
Eating seasonally is a cornerstone of embracing locally sourced ingredients. Explore the concept of seasonal eating and how it allows you to celebrate the unique flavors and bounties of each season. Discover the pleasure of anticipating the arrival of fresh produce, whether it's the first ripe strawberries in spring, the vibrant tomatoes of summer, or the hearty root vegetables of winter. Learn about the techniques of preserving and storing seasonal ingredients to enjoy their flavors throughout the year. Embrace the challenge of cooking with what's available locally and let the seasons inspire your gourmet creations.

Incorporating Locally Sourced Ingredients into Your Recipes
Once you have access to locally sourced ingredients, it's time to incorporate them into your recipes and let their flavors shine. Explore the techniques of highlighting the natural qualities of these ingredients, whether it's a simple salad that showcases fresh greens, a vibrant vegetable stir-fry, or a hearty stew made with locally raised meat. Discover the art of balancing flavors and textures while allowing the integrity of the ingredients to take center stage. Experiment with

recipes that highlight the unique characteristics of your local ingredients, creating dishes that are both delicious and deeply connected to your community.

Preserving the Harvest: Canning, Fermenting, and Freezing
To extend the enjoyment of locally sourced ingredients beyond their season, consider preserving the harvest through canning, fermenting, and freezing. Explore the techniques of making homemade jams, pickles, and sauces, capturing the flavors of peak-season produce to enjoy throughout the year. Learn about the art of fermentation, from sauerkraut to kimchi, as a way to preserve vegetables and enhance their flavors. Discover the methods of freezing fruits and vegetables to maintain their quality and nutritional value. By preserving the harvest, you can continue to enjoy the taste of locally sourced ingredients even when they are not readily available.

Conclusion:
Embracing locally sourced ingredients is not only about supporting local farmers and producers but also about enriching your culinary experiences. By understanding the importance of eating locally, building relationships with farmers, celebrating seasonal flavors, and incorporating these ingredients into your recipes, you can create a deeper connection between the food on your plate and the land it comes from. Embrace the farm-to-table movement and let the freshness, flavor, and sustainability of locally sourced ingredients inspire your gourmet cooking. Discover the joys of discovering new flavors, supporting your local food community, and nurturing a more conscious and sustainable approach to food.

Chapter 15

Culinary Fusion: Exploring Global Gourmet Flavors

Culinary fusion is a creative and dynamic approach to cooking that combines elements of different culinary traditions and flavors to create exciting and innovative dishes. In this chapter, we delve into the world of culinary fusion, exploring the richness of global gourmet flavors and the art of combining them harmoniously. From understanding the principles of fusion cuisine to exploring unique combinations and techniques, this chapter will inspire you to embark on a culinary adventure that transcends borders and creates delightful taste experiences.

The Essence of Culinary Fusion: Blending Traditions and Flavors
Culinary fusion is all about blending traditions and flavors from different culinary backgrounds to create something new and exciting. Explore the essence of culinary fusion and its history, which can be traced back to cultural exchange, migration, and trade routes. Learn about the principles of successful fusion cuisine, including understanding the flavor profiles of different cuisines, identifying complementary ingredients, and embracing creativity in the kitchen. Embrace the spirit of culinary exploration as you combine elements from various culinary traditions to create dishes that are greater than the sum of their parts.

Exploring Global Gourmet Flavors: A World of Culinary Inspiration
The world is a treasure trove of culinary traditions, each with its own unique flavors and techniques. Dive into the exploration of global gourmet flavors, discovering the spices,

herbs, condiments, and cooking techniques that define different cuisines. From the vibrant and bold spices of Indian cuisine to the delicate balance of flavors in Japanese dishes, and from the aromatic herbs of Mediterranean cooking to the fiery heat of Mexican cuisine, there is a wealth of inspiration to draw upon. Expand your flavor repertoire by incorporating elements of global cuisine into your culinary creations, adding depth and complexity to your dishes.

Unique Combinations: Creating Harmonious Fusions
The art of culinary fusion lies in creating harmonious combinations that blend different flavors seamlessly. Explore the techniques of combining ingredients from diverse culinary traditions, considering their complementary qualities and the balance of taste, texture, and aroma. Experiment with unique combinations, such as pairing Asian flavors with Latin American ingredients or infusing Mediterranean herbs into traditional Asian dishes. Embrace the unexpected and let your creativity guide you as you create exciting and memorable fusions that surprise and delight the palate.

Techniques of Fusion Cooking: Merging Culinary Methods
Fusion cooking goes beyond combining flavors; it also involves merging culinary techniques from different traditions. Learn about the techniques of fusion cooking, such as incorporating stir-frying methods into traditional French dishes or using traditional Indian spices in classic Italian recipes. Explore the art of adapting cooking methods to create new textures and flavors, and experiment with techniques like braising, grilling, and steaming to infuse dishes with a fusion twist. Embrace the versatility of culinary techniques and let them inspire your culinary creations.

Fusion Street Food: Global Flavors on the Go

Street food has always been a reflection of cultural fusion, as it evolves and adapts with each region's influences. Discover the world of fusion street food, where global flavors come together in handheld delights. Explore the diverse range of street food, from Mexican-inspired Korean tacos to Indian-inspired British curries, and from Vietnamese-inspired French banh mi to Middle Eastern-inspired Mexican shawarma. Learn about the techniques and ingredients that give these street food creations their unique flair, and experiment with bringing the vibrant flavors of global street food into your own kitchen.

Conclusion:
Culinary fusion opens up a world of possibilities, where flavors and traditions blend to create exciting and innovative dishes. By exploring global gourmet flavors, embracing unique combinations, and merging culinary techniques, you can embark on a culinary adventure that transcends borders and creates delightful taste experiences. Embrace the spirit of culinary exploration, draw inspiration from diverse culinary traditions, and let your creativity guide you as you infuse your dishes with the richness and complexity of fusion cuisine. By celebrating global flavors, you not only expand your culinary horizons but also foster a deeper appreciation for the diverse world of gastronomy.

Chapter 16

Sweet Temptations: Mastering Gourmet Desserts

Desserts are the crowning glory of a meal, the sweet finale that leaves a lasting impression. In this chapter, we delve into the art of mastering gourmet desserts, where creativity, technique, and a touch of indulgence come together to create sweet temptations that delight the senses. From understanding the foundations of pastry and baking to exploring the world of decadent confections and elegant desserts, this chapter will inspire you to elevate your dessert-making skills and create show-stopping treats that will leave your guests craving more.

The Art of Pastry and Baking: Building a Strong Foundation

Mastering gourmet desserts begins with a strong foundation in pastry and baking techniques. Explore the art of pastry-making, from the delicate balance of ingredients in a flaky pie crust to the precision of laminated doughs for croissants and puff pastries. Dive into the world of baking, learning the science behind perfect cakes, cookies, and breads. Understand the importance of measuring accurately, controlling temperatures, and mastering the art of dough handling. With a solid understanding of pastry and baking fundamentals, you can confidently create a wide array of exquisite desserts.

Decadent Confections: Indulging in Sweet Delights

Indulge in the world of decadent confections, where sweetness and richness take center stage. Discover the techniques of creating luxurious chocolates, from hand-tempering to molding and filling. Learn the art of crafting perfect caramels, with their luscious texture and deep flavors.

Dive into the realm of creamy, silky truffles and velvety fudges, experimenting with different flavors and textures. Explore the world of sweet temptations, from buttery toffees to delicate macarons, and let your creativity shine as you create confections that are truly irresistible.

Elegant Desserts: A Symphony of Flavors and Presentation
Elevate your dessert-making skills with elegant creations that marry flavors, textures, and presentation. Discover the art of creating balanced flavor profiles, combining ingredients that harmonize and contrast in delightful ways. Experiment with different textures, from crunchy meringues to smooth custards and silky mousses. Explore the techniques of assembling and decorating desserts, creating visual masterpieces that are as beautiful as they are delicious. From multi-layered cakes to individual plated desserts, let your imagination run wild and create desserts that are works of art.

Seasonal and Fruit-Based Desserts: Embracing Nature's Bounty
Celebrate the seasons and embrace the natural sweetness of fruits in your gourmet desserts. Explore the possibilities of seasonal desserts, using fresh berries in summer tarts, pumpkin and spices in autumn pies, and citrus fruits in refreshing winter sorbets. Learn the techniques of preserving fruits to enjoy their flavors all year round, from jams and compotes to fruit-infused syrups. Experiment with unique flavor combinations, such as pairing tropical fruits with aromatic herbs or incorporating exotic spices into fruit-based desserts. Let nature's bounty inspire your creations and bring a touch of freshness and vibrancy to your sweet temptations.

Artful Plating and Dessert Presentation: Creating Memorable Experiences

Desserts not only satisfy our taste buds but also captivate our eyes. Explore the art of dessert plating and presentation, creating memorable experiences for your guests. Learn about the principles of balance, symmetry, and color in dessert plating. Discover the techniques of creating intricate designs with sauces, garnishes, and edible decorations. Experiment with different serving vessels, from elegant dessert plates to whimsical glassware and creative individual portions. Elevate your desserts from mere sweet treats to artistic expressions that delight all the senses.

Conclusion:
Mastering gourmet desserts is a journey of creativity, precision, and indulgence. By building a strong foundation in pastry and baking techniques, exploring the world of decadent confections, and creating elegant desserts that marry flavors and presentation, you can create sweet temptations that leave a lasting impression. Embrace the art of dessert-making, experiment with unique flavor combinations, and let your creativity soar as you create desserts that are as beautiful as they are delicious. Whether you're creating a simple fruit tart or an elaborate multi-component dessert, the joy of mastering gourmet desserts lies in the pleasure they bring to both the creator and the lucky individuals who get to savor each sweet bite.

Chapter 17

Artful Baking: Pies, Tarts, and Pastries

Baking is an art form that brings together precision, technique, and creativity. In this chapter, we explore the world of artful baking, focusing specifically on pies, tarts, and pastries. These delectable treats not only tantalize our taste buds but also captivate our eyes with their beautifully crafted crusts, luscious fillings, and intricate designs. Join us as we dive into the art of creating stunning pies, elegant tarts, and delicate pastries that will make you the star baker in any gathering.

The Art of Pie-Making: Perfecting Crusts and Fillings
Pie-making is a cherished tradition that spans cultures and generations. Discover the art of creating the perfect pie crust, from flaky and buttery to tender and crumbly. Learn the secrets to achieving a golden, crisp crust that complements your choice of fillings. Explore a variety of pie fillings, from classic fruit combinations to rich custards and savory options. Master the techniques of blind baking, lattice tops, decorative crusts, and beautiful crimping. With precision and practice, you can create pies that are as stunning as they are delicious.

Elegant Tarts: Showcasing Seasonal Fruits and Creamy Fillings
Tarts are the epitome of elegance, with their buttery pastry shells and exquisite fillings. Delve into the world of elegant tarts, where seasonal fruits take center stage and creamy custards create a velvety indulgence. Explore the techniques of creating a perfect tart shell, from patting the dough into the pan to blind baking for a crisp base. Experiment with various fillings, from fresh berries and stone fruits to silky chocolate ganache and tangy lemon curd. Discover the art of arranging

fruit slices in beautiful patterns and using decorative piping to add visual appeal. With each tart, you have the opportunity to create a miniature masterpiece.

Delicate Pastries: Layers of Flaky Goodness

Pastries are a testament to the patience and skill of a baker. Uncover the art of creating delicate pastries, with their layers of flaky goodness. Learn the technique of laminating dough to create croissants, puff pastries, and Danish pastries. Master the balance between crispiness and tenderness, as you work with buttery doughs that rise to perfection. Discover the joy of creating palmiers, turnovers, and cream-filled delights. Explore flavor combinations, from savory options like cheese and herbs to sweet fillings like almond paste and fruit compote. Each bite of a perfectly baked pastry is an experience that delights the senses.

Artful Presentation: Making Your Bakes Visually Stunning

Baking is not just about taste; it's also about presentation. Discover the art of making your bakes visually stunning. Learn how to create decorative pie crusts using intricate cutouts, braids, and lattice patterns. Explore the techniques of glazing tarts with a glossy finish, arranging fruits in captivating designs, and dusting pastries with a delicate sprinkle of powdered sugar. Consider the use of edible flowers, herbs, and other decorative elements to add a touch of elegance to your creations. Let your imagination soar as you transform your bakes into edible works of art.

Conclusion:

Artful baking is a delightful blend of precision, technique, and creativity. By mastering the art of pie-making, creating elegant tarts, and crafting delicate pastries, you can bring joy to both your taste buds and your eyes. Embrace the opportunity to create stunning crusts, experiment with flavorful fillings, and let your artistic side shine through in your presentation. With each bake, you have the chance to transport your guests to a world of delectable delights. So, roll up your sleeves, dust off your rolling pin, and embark on a baking adventure that will elevate your skills and leave a lasting impression.

Chapter 18

Chocolatier's Delight: Crafting Divine Chocolate Creations

Chocolate has long been hailed as the epitome of indulgence and pleasure. In this chapter, we explore the enchanting world of chocolate and the art of being a chocolatier. From understanding the origins and varieties of chocolate to mastering the techniques of tempering, molding, and decorating, we delve into the secrets of creating divine chocolate creations. Whether you're a passionate home cook or an aspiring professional, join us on this delectable journey as we unlock the mysteries of working with chocolate and craft irresistible treats that will make your taste buds dance with delight.

The Magic of Chocolate: A Journey from Bean to Bar
To truly appreciate the art of chocolate-making, it's essential to understand its origins. Explore the journey of chocolate, from the cacao tree to the transformation of cacao beans into luscious chocolate. Learn about the different varieties of cacao and the flavor profiles they bring. Discover the process of harvesting, fermenting, and roasting cacao beans to unlock their unique flavors. Dive into the world of chocolate production, from bean-to-bar artisans to large-scale manufacturing. Gain a deeper appreciation for the magic of chocolate and how it captivates our senses.

Tempering: The Key to Perfectly Smooth and Shiny Chocolate
Tempering is a crucial technique in chocolate work, ensuring that chocolate sets with a smooth and glossy finish. Explore the art of tempering chocolate, from understanding the science behind it to mastering the different methods. Learn

how to control temperatures, manipulate the crystal structure of chocolate, and achieve the perfect consistency for dipping, molding, and coating. With proper tempering, you can create professional-quality chocolate creations that are visually stunning and have that irresistible snap and texture.

Molding and Sculpting: Creating Beautiful Chocolate Shapes

Unleash your creativity as you learn the art of molding and sculpting chocolate. Discover the techniques of creating stunning chocolate shapes, from simple bonbons and truffles to intricate molded figurines and showpieces. Explore the world of chocolate molds, understanding their types and uses. Learn how to properly fill and release chocolate from molds, ensuring clean lines and perfect details. Delve into the art of hand sculpting with chocolate, shaping delicate flowers, elegant decorations, and personalized designs. Let your imagination run wild as you bring your chocolate creations to life.

Ganaches, Pralines, and Fillings: Infusing Flavors into Chocolate

The marriage of chocolate and fillings is a match made in heaven. Dive into the realm of ganaches, pralines, and fillings, discovering the art of infusing flavors into chocolate. Learn the techniques of creating silky-smooth ganaches, from classic flavors like dark chocolate and raspberry to more adventurous combinations like chili and lime. Experiment with pralines, blending roasted nuts with caramelized sugar and chocolate for a delightful crunch. Explore the art of incorporating fruits, spices, herbs, and liqueurs into fillings, creating a symphony of flavors that complement the richness of chocolate. Let your taste buds guide you as you create heavenly combinations.

Chocolate Decorations: Adding Elegance and Flair

Elevate your chocolate creations by mastering the art of chocolate decorations. Discover the techniques of creating delicate chocolate curls, shavings, and shards. Learn how to make intricate chocolate lattice designs and piped decorations. Explore the world of chocolate transfers, using edible sheets to transfer intricate patterns and images onto your chocolates. Experiment with dusting, airbrushing, and hand-painted designs to add flair and artistic touches. With each decoration, you have the opportunity to transform your chocolate creations into edible masterpieces.

Conclusion:
Being a chocolatier is a journey of passion, precision, and pure indulgence. By understanding the origins and varieties of chocolate, mastering the art of tempering, molding, and decorating, and infusing flavors into chocolate, you can create divine chocolate creations that will enchant and delight. Whether you're crafting simple bonbons or elaborate showpieces, the joy of working with chocolate lies in the alchemy of transforming humble ingredients into irresistible treats. So, embrace the magic of chocolate, let your creativity soar, and indulge in the sweet satisfaction of being a chocolatier.

Chapter 19

Gourmet Entertaining: Hosting Memorable Dinner Parties

Hosting a dinner party is an art form that combines culinary prowess, gracious hospitality, and an eye for detail. In this chapter, we delve into the realm of gourmet entertaining, where you will learn how to create unforgettable dining experiences for your guests. From planning the menu to setting the ambiance, we will guide you through the intricacies of hosting a memorable dinner party that will leave a lasting impression on your friends and loved ones. So, let's embark on this journey of culinary excellence and discover the secrets to becoming a master of gourmet entertaining.

Planning the Perfect Menu: Balancing Flavors and Courses
A well-crafted menu sets the stage for a memorable dining experience. Learn the art of planning a gourmet menu, considering flavor profiles, balance, and variety. Discover the secrets of creating a harmonious progression of courses, from elegant appetizers that awaken the palate to showstopping main dishes and indulgent desserts. Explore the interplay of textures, flavors, and presentation as you curate a menu that showcases your culinary expertise and delights your guests' taste buds.

Culinary Showmanship: Spectacular Plating and Presentation
Elevate your dinner parties to the realm of gourmet by mastering the art of culinary showmanship. Delve into the techniques of spectacular plating and presentation, where each dish becomes a work of art. Learn how to arrange

ingredients with precision, use edible garnishes to add visual appeal, and create stunning plate compositions that showcase your culinary skills. Discover the secrets of balancing colors, textures, and heights to create visually striking dishes that will wow your guests.

Wine Pairing: Enhancing Flavors and Elevating the Dining Experience

A carefully selected wine can elevate a meal from good to extraordinary. Explore the art of wine pairing, where flavors harmonize and enhance each other. Learn the fundamentals of pairing wine with different courses, understanding the nuances of acidity, tannins, and sweetness. Discover the characteristics of different wine varietals and how they complement various dishes. Whether it's a full-bodied red with a perfectly seared steak or a crisp white with delicate seafood, master the art of wine pairing to create a truly memorable dining experience for your guests.

Tablescaping: Creating Ambiance and Elegance

The ambiance of your dining space sets the tone for the entire evening. Delve into the art of tablescaping, where creativity and attention to detail transform a table into a visual masterpiece. Learn how to choose the right table linens, select elegant dinnerware and glassware, and create captivating centerpieces that reflect the theme and mood of the occasion. Explore the use of lighting, candles, and decorative elements to create a warm and inviting atmosphere. With thoughtful tablescaping, you can create a dining experience that is both visually stunning and memorable.

Effortless Hosting: Managing Timing and Guest Experience

Being a gracious host goes beyond the culinary aspect of entertaining. Master the art of effortless hosting by managing timing and ensuring a seamless guest experience. Learn how to plan and execute a timeline for your dinner party, ensuring that dishes are served at their prime. Discover techniques for multitasking, staying organized, and enlisting the help of trusted assistants. Explore ways to make your guests feel welcome and comfortable, from greeting them with a signature cocktail to engaging in lively conversation. By attending to the finer details of hosting, you can create an atmosphere of warmth and hospitality that will leave a lasting impression.

Conclusion:
Gourmet entertaining is an intricate dance of flavors, aesthetics, and hospitality. By planning the perfect menu, mastering the art of culinary showmanship, understanding the nuances of wine pairing, creating an ambiance of elegance through tablescaping, and effortlessly hosting your guests, you can create memorable dinner parties that will be talked about long after the last bite has been savored. So, let your culinary creativity shine, embrace the joy of hosting, and create moments of pure delight for your guests as you become a master of gourmet entertaining.

Chapter 20

The Art of Food Presentation: Plating Techniques and Garnishes

Food presentation is an integral part of the dining experience. The way a dish is presented not only affects its visual appeal but also enhances the overall enjoyment of the meal. In this chapter, we explore the art of food presentation, delving into plating techniques and garnishes that elevate a dish from ordinary to extraordinary. From understanding the principles of composition to learning the art of balancing colors, textures, and heights, we will guide you through the secrets of creating visually stunning plates that tantalize the senses. So, let's embark on this culinary journey and uncover the art of food presentation.

The Principles of Composition: Creating Balanced and Harmonious Plates

Understanding the principles of composition is fundamental to creating visually appealing plates. Explore the elements of design, such as balance, symmetry, and asymmetry, and how they can be applied to food presentation. Learn how to use negative space to enhance the focal point of a dish and create visual interest. Discover the power of color, texture, and shape in creating dynamic and harmonious compositions. By mastering the principles of composition, you can transform a plate into a canvas of culinary art.

Plating Techniques: From Classic to Contemporary

Plating techniques play a vital role in creating visually striking dishes. Explore a range of plating techniques, from classic to contemporary, and understand how each style can enhance the presentation of different types of dishes. Learn the art of stacking, layering, and arranging ingredients to create depth and visual interest. Discover the techniques of using molds and rings to create clean and precise shapes. Experiment with swooshes, drizzles, and dots to add artistic flair to your plates. With a repertoire of plating techniques at your disposal, you can turn any dish into a masterpiece.

Balancing Colors and Textures: Creating Visual Harmony
Color and texture are essential components of food presentation. Learn how to balance colors to create visually appealing plates that stimulate the appetite. Explore the use of complementary and contrasting colors to create dynamic and eye-catching presentations. Discover the impact of texture on the overall visual experience, from crisp and crunchy to smooth and creamy. Master the art of incorporating different textures in a dish to create contrast and add visual interest. By understanding the interplay of colors and textures, you can create plates that are not only visually stunning but also enticing to the palate.

Garnishes: Edible Artistry and Flavor Enhancements
Garnishes are the finishing touch that adds a touch of artistry and flavor to a dish. Explore the world of garnishes, from delicate herb sprigs and edible flowers to vibrant sauces and flavorful oils. Learn how to use garnishes to enhance the visual appeal of a dish, adding pops of color, texture, and dimension. Discover the techniques of creating decorative cuts, such as chiffonades and julienne, to elevate the presentation of ingredients. Understand the balance between garnishes and the main components of a dish, ensuring that they complement each other in both flavor and visual impact. With creative and thoughtful garnishing, you can elevate a simple plate of food into a culinary masterpiece.

Edible Centerpieces: Taking Presentation to the Next Level

Creating edible centerpieces adds a wow factor to your food presentation. Delve into the art of sculpting, molding, and crafting show-stopping edible centerpieces. Learn how to create edible sculptures from ingredients such as fruits, vegetables, and chocolate. Discover the techniques of using sugar and isomalt to create intricate sugar art that dazzles the eye. Explore the world of edible decorations, from spun sugar to pulled sugar and delicate chocolate work. With edible centerpieces, you can create a focal point on the table that will leave your guests in awe.

Conclusion:
Food presentation is an art form that allows you to express your creativity, passion, and attention to detail. By understanding the principles of composition, mastering plating techniques, balancing colors and textures, utilizing garnishes, and creating edible centerpieces, you can transform a simple dish into a visual masterpiece. So, let your culinary creativity soar, experiment with different techniques and garnishes, and create plates that not only delight the taste buds but also captivate the eyes. Embrace the art of food presentation and elevate your culinary creations to new heights of aesthetic excellence.

Printed in the USA
CPSIA information can be obtained
at www.ICGtesting.com
LVHW010304291223
767719LV00038B/1000